ON THE SHUTTLE

EIGHT DAYS IN SPACE

BY BARBARA BONDAR
WITH DR. ROBERTA BONDAR

Greey de Pencier Books

This book is dedicated
with love and admiration to Sonny Carter,
astronaut, navy captain, doctor, pilot.

It is hoped that this book will continue Sonny's excitement about life and
space and his commitment to young people and their education.

We have been touched by his greatness.

Books from OWL are published by Greey de Pencier Books,
179 John St., Suite 500, Toronto, Ontario M5T 3G5.

*OWL and the OWL colophon are trademarks of the Young Naturalist Foundation.
Greey de Pencier Books is a licensed user of trademarks of the Young Naturalist
Foundation.

Published simultaneously in the United States by Firefly Books (U.S.) Inc.,
230 Fifth Ave., Suite 1607, New York, NY 10001.

IMAX® is a registered trademark of the IMAX Corporation, Toronto, Canada.

This book was published with the generous support of the Canada Council,
the Ontario Arts Council and the Ontario Ministry of Culture and Communications.

Canadian Cataloguing in Publication Data

Bondar, Barbara, 1944—
On the shuttle: eight days in space

ISBN 1-895688-12-4 (bound) ISBN 1-895688-10-8 (pbk.)

1. Bondar, R. L. (Roberta L.), 1945— - Juvenile
literature. 2. Space shuttles - Juvenile
literature. 3. Women astronauts - Canada -
Biography - Juvenile literature. 4. Astronauts -
Canada - Biography - Juvenile literature. I. Title.

TL789.85.B65B65 1993   j629.45'0092   C93-093484-9

Design and art direction: Julia Naimska
Cover photography: IMAX photo, ©Smithsonian Institution/Lockheed Corporation 1992
Back cover photography: (top) W. Stephen Cooper, NASA

Printed in Hong Kong

C   D   E   F   G   H

The author is grateful to:
Dr. Roberta L. Bondar, who can zero in on a subject with her sharp intellect, and who,
as always, talked me into one more project, this one;

Our parents, Mildred and Edward Bondar, who raised two energetic, inquisitive kids. On
this project their influence was felt from the preface photograph, taken so many years
ago, to the organization of the manuscript files;

Lauretta Anonby, President, Merritt Maclean Inc., who, for three years, arranged my
computer programming workload to give me large blocks of time in which to write.

Special thanks to:
Joyce Lees & BGM Colour Labs staff, Graeme and Phyllis Ferguson, IMAX Systems Corpo-
ration, Eleanor Koldofsky, Brent Lavictoire, Flo Stein, Lisa Vazquez, Lise Beaudoin, Patsy
Bynum, Dr. Priscilla Galloway, Joellen J. Lashbrook, Robert O. McBrayer, Marian and
Gordon Penrose, Barbara L. Present, Dr. Betty I. Roots, Paul Stampfl, Dr. Roger Crouch,
Colonel Ronald J. and Marijo Grabe, Colonel David C. and Lynn Hilmers, Dr. Ulf and
Birgit Merbold, Dr. Kenneth Money, Stephen S. and Diane Oswald, Mr. William F. Readdy
and Colleen Nevius, Dr. Norman E. and Kirby Thagard.

Photo and Illustration Credits
NASA — 2, 5 (W. Stephen Cooper), 7 bottom, 8 top (MSFC), 9, 10 (W. Stephen Cooper),
11 bottom, 12, 13, 14 top, 16, 17, 19 bottom, 20, 22, 23, 27, 28 top and center,
29 top, 30 (courtesy of Tina Melton, MSFC), 32 top (W. Stephen Cooper), 32–33, 34,
35 (JSC), 37 right (Emmett L. Given/MSFC), 38, 39, 40, 41, 43, 46, 47 top, 47 bottom
(W. Stephen Cooper), 48, 50, 51 bottom right, 52, 53 (Emmett L. Given/MSFC), 55 top
(MSFC), 56, 57, 58–59, 60; IMAX photos, ©Smithsonian Institution/Lockheed Corporation 1992 — 3, 24 top and bottom, 29 bottom, 31, 36, 42, 45, 50 top, 51 left and
top right, 54–55; Edward Bondar — 4; Dr. Roberta Bondar — 6, 21, 49 bottom right
and left; Graeme Walker — 7 top, 8 bottom, 19 top, 25 center, 26, 33, 62; The Orlan-
do Sentinel — 11 top; Michael R. Brown/Florida Today — 14–15; Vesna Krstanovich —
18, 49 top; IMAX/W. Stephen Cooper — 28 bottom; CEN (Beysens) for ESA — 37 left;
CSA/W. Stephen Cooper — 50 inset; Alexandra Smith/University of Guelph, Dept. of Food
Science — 54 top; Dr. Betty I. Roots — 61; Lynn Hilmers — 63.

CONTENTS

DREAMS OF SPACE

Two sisters hide together under a large walnut dining table. Scarcely breathing, they listen to footsteps disappearing down the corridor of an alien space station.

No, the children aren't imagining things. It is another Saturday morning and, as usual, they are glued to the radio in front of them. As large as a jukebox and with glowing dials, the radio enthralls the two with the exciting adventures of Commander Tom and Cadet Happy.

When the radio show is over, the sisters will probably spend the rest of the day outside, finishing off their model spaceship of wood and cardboard, complete with wire cockpit

Roberta and Barbara Bondar looking to the future.

controls. The cardboard space helmets they received by writing away to the bubble gum company are standing by, ready for the launch.

And 35 years later? Well, one of the sisters will fly in a real spaceship — and the other will record the real adventure in this book.

THE FIRST INTERNATIONAL MICROGRAVITY LABORATORY

A QUESTION OF GRAVITY

Why did six major international space research organizations and over 200 scientists from 14 countries work together for years to make the first International Microgravity Laboratory mission a success? Quite simply, they were looking for answers. The scientists hope that experiments carried out on *Discovery* and on future missions will help them answer the question: "How do things behave without gravity?" The answers not only will help them learn more about life in space, but will help them understand better how things work right here on Earth, too.

◆ Each shuttle flight is special. Each mission adds new information to what we know about ourselves, our planet and our universe. This book is about one particular journey into orbit around Earth. It is about the *Discovery* mission that began on January 22, 1992.

This mission was the first flight of the International Microgravity Laboratory (IML-1), the first in a series of flights that carried out the experiments of many scientists from around the world. On board *Discovery* were three orbiter crew (in charge of flying the shuttle), four specialists — and lots of unusual baggage, such as oat and wheat seeds, hamsters, mice, frogs and crystals, to name a few. Also on board was an amazing laboratory called Spacelab. There is less gravity in a space shuttle orbiting Earth than there is on the planet itself, and Spacelab is where the scientists are able to experiment with the effects of this unnatural microgravity on everything from people

to liquids. The results of these experiments help scientists learn more about life in space and about life here on Earth, too.

And life on board a shuttle is like nothing you could ever imagine. Everything the astronauts do, from eating to sleeping to doing scientific experiments, is a challenge. So hold onto your seat as we explore the preparation and flight of IML-1 and its exciting cargo — from blast-off to touchdown!

◆ Every shuttle mission has a specific patch, like the one shown above. Throughout this book you'll see other patches, which represent many of the scientific experiments on board IML-1. Each patch was designed by the scientists in charge of those particular experiments.

READYING DISCOVERY

◆ After its previous mission in space, the orbiter *Discovery* landed at Edwards Air Force Base in California. Months before our mission's launch date, the orbiter was attached or "mated" to a Boeing 747 airplane and flown across the country from California to Cape Canaveral, Florida, where repairs and preparations for its 14th flight began.

Since an orbiter can't fly on its own, it must hitch a ride on a Boeing 747 to get from its landing place to its next launch site.

THE POWER OF LIFT-OFF

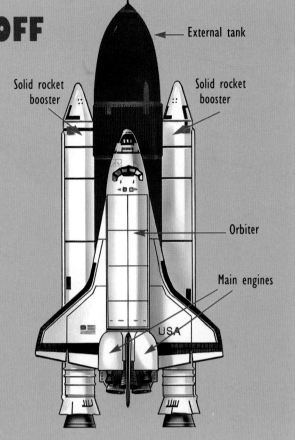

External tank

Solid rocket booster

Solid rocket booster

Orbiter

Main engines

USA

At launch a space shuttle is made up of three main components. The orbiter is the part of the shuttle that houses the crew and the cargo compartments. It is the part of the shuttle that orbits the Earth and then returns to the launch pad.

The orbiter is piggybacked into space on a huge fuel tank called the external tank, which is filled with liquid hydrogen and liquid oxygen. This tank fuels the engines at the rear of the orbiter during launching.

On two sides of the external fuel tank are large cylinders called solid rocket boosters. They are filled with solid fuel and have engines of their own. It is the solid rocket boosters and the extra fuel from the huge external tank that generate enough energy to lift the shuttle into space.

When the shuttle is leaving the Earth's atmosphere, the solid rocket boosters fall back to Earth and can be picked up and refilled to help lift another orbiter into space. The external tank, however, falls off later and is almost totally destroyed by heat and friction as it falls back through Earth's atmosphere.

◆ With only 41 days left before *Discovery* is launched, the orbiter is attached to the solid rocket boosters and the huge external fuel tank, which is much bigger than the orbiter itself. The fuel tank is empty for now. On launch day, the liquid fuel will be pumped into the tank. The great quantity of liquid fuel inside the tank supplies the shuttle with power for only eight minutes, but that's all the time it takes to carry the shuttle out of the Earth's atmosphere.

From above, *Discovery* is lowered into position with the external tank and the solid rocket boosters.

IML-1: INSIDE THE SHUTTLE

The long middle part of the shuttle is called the Payload Bay. Whatever goes in this area is what "pays" for the flight, or is the reason for the mission.

The front section of the shuttle is divided into three floors called the flight deck, the mid-deck and the lower deck.

The payload on this mission is the International Microgravity Laboratory. Most of the IML-1 experiments are contained in the rounded tent-like structure called Spacelab.

The tall fin-like wing above the rockets is the vertical stabilizer. It helps keep the shuttle on course.

Behind Spacelab in the Payload Bay are the Get Away Special canisters, which contain other, unattended experiments.

To get to Spacelab, the scientists go through a pressurized tunnel that starts in the mid-deck.

The Payload Bay doors open along the top of the shuttle to allow the payload to be loaded. These doors can also be opened while the shuttle is on orbit.

Three main engine nozzles at the rear burn the fuel from the external tank during lift-off. The Orbital Maneuvering System, also at the rear, is used to maneuver the shuttle in space.

Commander's seat

Pilot's seat

Sleep stations

Storage lockers

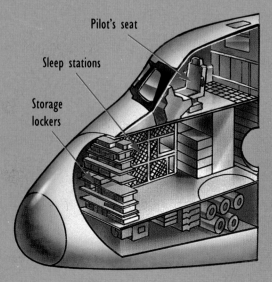

From the flight deck, the crew control the flight and orbit of the shuttle. Through the front and rear flight deck windows, they can take pictures of the Earth and the shuttle itself.

Mid-deck houses the sleep stations, food lockers, washroom facilities and storage lockers.

More storage room is found in the lower deck.

PACKING LIGHT

Have you ever packed a suitcase or a knapsack to take on a trip? Do you find there never seems to be enough room to take everything that you want? It's the same on the shuttle. And not only is room scarce, but keeping the weight to a minimum is important, too.

That's why every single item that goes into a shuttle has to be carefully planned, weighed and packed. Several years ago, food scientists and other engineers developed the pull ring that is common today on pet food and other cans. It is small and flat, can be used on all cans — and it means the astronauts don't have to pack a can opener!

On December 19th the assembled shuttle is rolled out to the launch pad. Later on, about two days before the launch, the orbiter's on-board fuel tanks are filled. Nine hours before the launch, the large external tank will be pumped full of liquid fuel.

SHUFFLING SHUTTLES

Originally the shuttle *Columbia* was picked for the IML-1 flight. Then, in 1991, it was taken out of service to be fitted out for longer space flights. *Discovery* was the next available orbiter, but by then the only flight times available on it were for seven-day missions, so the original ten-day IML-1 mission had to be shortened.*

When cracked hinges were discovered on *Discovery*, Spacelab was rescheduled to fly on the shuttle *Atlantis*. Then fuel leaks meant all flights scheduled on *Atlantis* were delayed. In the meantime, *Discovery* was repaired.

The result? Spacelab flew on *Discovery*.

---

*Although IML-1 was rescheduled as a seven-day mission, on Day 04 it was decided to extend that time to eight days.

ON YOUR MARK

◆ The day of the launch has arrived. The shuttle is ready at the launch pad. And the crew? They have been awake since 3:00 this morning. They try to settle down enough to have a good breakfast together.

◆ It's 6:30 a.m. and time for the crew to suit up in the "clean room" of their quarantined quarters. It takes the astronauts about 20 minutes to put on most of the components of their launch/entry suits (LES). This suit will provide protection against the heat and pressure changes during lift-off. It will also provide the astronauts with an extra layer of protection from cold or fire in case of emergency.

◆ On their launch/entry suits the crew members proudly wear the official mission flight patch, which they designed.

KEEPING HEALTHY

Actually, the crew have been eating breakfast together for the past seven mornings. They've been kept secluded for the past week. Experiments performed on previous shuttle flights have shown that bacteria grown in microgravity are larger, grow faster and are more resistant to antibiotics than are bacteria on Earth. The Health Stabilization Program keeps the crew from acquiring disease from others and becoming ill in space.

Because it usually takes a bacterial infection seven days to show itself, seven days is the length of time the crew is quarantined. For seven days, the crew work, study and eat together in special facilities.

Everyone that could come in contact with them is first checked out by doctors so there is little chance of a crew member catching an infection from anyone. A badge like this one means the person may visit the crew without risk.

NASA
Space Transportation System
Health Stabilization Program

SPACE SHUTTLE

Barbara Bondar
STS—42 ONLY
Expires: _____

PRIMARY CONTACT

JSC Form 126C (Rev Apr 88)

A REAL SPACE SUIT

It's hard to move fast when you're wearing a launch/entry suit. All in all, the LES weighs a hefty 41 kg (90 lb.)! In addition to the outer suit, each made-to-measure LES consists of (clockwise from upper left) long underwear, communications hat, helmet, parachute, flotation device, gloves, inflatable lower back pad, inflatable seat support, boots, gravity pants (inside suit), socks, signalling device, diaper and diaper belt. Why the diaper? It's very uncomfortable to keep a full bladder under the extreme pressure of entry into orbit. Especially if you've been lying on your back for about three hours waiting for the end of the countdown.

After years of preparation, the IML-1 crew head for the shuttle. From left: William Readdy, Stephen Oswald, Norman Thagard, Ulf Merbold, David Hilmers, Roberta Bondar, Ronald Grabe.

◆ The crew walk outside to the van that waits to carry them to the launch pad. The walkout is the last point at which carefully screened observers with special passes, such as television and newspaper reporters, may see the crew.

Flying in a shuttle requires years of training and hard work. Each member of the shuttle crew has special skills — and special responsibilities.

The astronauts responsible for operating the shuttle and keeping the crew safe are called the orbiter crew. The orbiter crew are members of the astronaut corps of the U.S. National Aeronautics and Space Administration (NASA). They are the commander, the pilot and the flight engineer. They were picked for this flight a year before launch.

The rest of the crew are specialists. The Mission Specialists are astronauts who are responsible for on-board maintenance of the orbiter and Spacelab systems and equipment. The Payload Specialists are responsible for the science experiments. They have been training together for three years to prepare for this brief shuttle mission.

As the van carries them to the launch pad, meet the crew of this space shuttle mission.

Commander Ronald Grabe

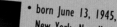

- born June 13, 1945, New York, New York
- Colonel, United States Air Force
- NASA astronaut
- Third shuttle flight
- B.S. in engineering science
- combat fighter pilot, test pilot, test pilot instructor

Pilot Stephen Oswald

- born June 30, 1951, Seattle, Washington
- Commanding Officer, Naval Space Command Reserve Unit
- NASA astronaut
- First shuttle flight
- B.S. in aerospace engineering
- test pilot, flight instructor, flight software verifier

Flight Engineer William Readdy

- born January 24, 1952, Quonset Point, Rhode Island
- Commander, United States Naval Reserve
- NASA astronaut
- First shuttle flight
- B.S. in aeronautical engineering
- test pilot, test pilot instructor

Mission Specialist Norman Thagard

- born July 3, 1943, Marianna, Florida
- former Captain, United States Marine Corps Reserve
- NASA astronaut
- Fourth shuttle flight
- B.S., M.S. in engineering science, M.D.
- naval aviator, researcher, teacher

Mission Specialist David Hilmers

- born January 28, 1950, Clinton, Iowa
- Lieutenant Colonel, United States Marine Corps
- NASA astronaut
- Fourth shuttle flight
- B.S. in mathematics, M.S. in electrical engineering
- pilot

Payload Specialist Roberta Bondar

- born December 4, 1945, Sault Ste. Marie, Ontario
- Canadian Space Agency astronaut
- First shuttle flight
- B.S. in zoology and agriculture, M.S. in experimental pathology, Ph.D. in neurobiology, M.D.
- pilot, neurologist, Principal Investigator on IML-1 taste experiments, researcher in cerebral blood flow during weightlessness and readaptation to Earth

Payload Specialist Ulf Merbold

- born June 20, 1941, Greiz, Germany
- European Space Agency astronaut
- Second shuttle flight
- B.A., Ph.D. in physics
- head of German Aerospace Research Establishment, pilot, researcher, Principal Investigator on IML-1 solid state and low-temperature physics experiments

SONNY CARTER

NASA astronaut Manley "Sonny" Carter, Jr., was chosen to be a Mission Specialist on the IML-1 mission. This would have been his second shuttle flight, but on April 5, 1991, he was killed in a commercial airline accident. Having trained together for nearly a year, the team of seven astronauts had grown very close. They were shocked and saddened by the death of their friend and colleague. Dave Hilmers then joined the crew as the replacement Mission Specialist.

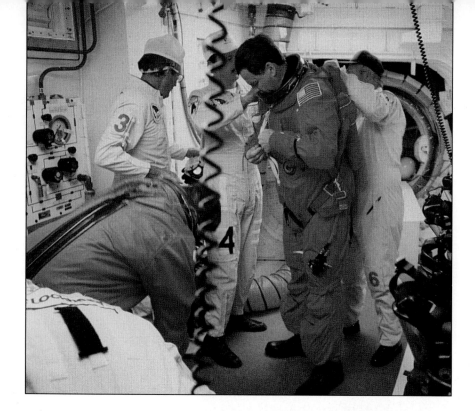

◆ As the time of the launch approaches, the air becomes charged with suspense and excitement. With only a few hours remaining, the van drives the crew to the crane-like gantry that holds the assembled space shuttle.

◆ The crew ride up the elevator 60 m (195 ft.) to the gantry "white room." There, the crew members put on the rest of their launch/entry suits: the parachute harness, communications hat, helmet and gloves.

◆ About this time, the guests and families of the crew are being assembled at a private viewing site about 5 km (3 mi.) away from the launch site.

◆ Each of the astronauts in turn is strapped into place on board *Discovery* by the gantry flight crew. They lie on their backs with their knees pointing towards the sky. The Payload Specialists, Merbold and Bondar, and one of the Mission Specialists are located in three chairs in the mid-deck. Their chairs are called take-down chairs since they will be folded up and stored out of the way after the launch. Commander Grabe and Pilot Oswald are strapped into their seats in the flight deck. Flight engineer Readdy, who is also the navigator, and the second Mission Specialist are strapped into take-down chairs that are located just behind the commander and pilot in the flight deck.

◆ The orbiter crew concentrate on following the lift-off checklist, which is broadcast to them through their communications helmets. Everyone in the launch viewing site watches the countdown on the large electronic clock. Family members hold hands and wrap their arms about one another in silence.

◆ The countdown reaches zero. It is 9:53 in the morning. The three main orbiter engines try to lift more than 1.75 million kilograms (4 million pounds) from the pad. The shuttle shifts slightly.

A few seconds later, the ignition process for the solid rocket boosters begins. With a loud, low rumble the shuttle stirs to life. Inside their helmets, the crew hear voices from the ground, double-checking the lift-off procedures.

◆ Suddenly there is lift-off as the solid rocket boosters ignite. The loud roar of the shuttle engines fills the air.

As the shuttle lifts off, jets of water spray out to cool the launch tower and dampen the powerful shock waves. Enormous clouds of water vapor engulf the launch site.

WE HAVE LIFT-OFF!

JUST IN CASE

If the shuttle's main engines fail, the orbiter crew can land the shuttle at one of eight emergency landing sites in Africa and Europe, depending on when the problem arises. If *Discovery* had to land suddenly soon after lift-off, they would go to the emergency site in Morocco. This view of the Straits of Gibraltar is what the commander and pilot would see from the windows in the flight deck.

◆ When the shuttle blasts free of the gantry, the *Discovery* astronauts begin their skyward journey. It is a bone-jolting, shake-rattle-and-roll ride. It feels like they are going up and up, faster and faster, on a monster roller-coaster.

◆ Two minutes and six seconds after lift-off, the solid rocket boosters separate from the shuttle and the ride becomes smoother.

Now all that is propelling the shuttle into space is the main engines, fueled by the external tank. In the last 45 seconds before the main engines cut off as the shuttle fights to break free of gravity, the crew feel the maximum 3 Gs of entry into orbit. What does that feel like? Imagine lying on your back with a full-grown gorilla sitting on your chest!

◆ Eight minutes after launch, the shuttle has reached a height of 296 km (184 mi.) above the Earth. The main engines stop firing and the large external tank separates and falls away. The Orbital Maneuvering System engines are fired to correctly position the shuttle in space. *Discovery* is on orbit.

◆ All three members of the orbiter crew were chosen over a year ago for this flight. They have been looking forward to this moment for a long time. This is Commander Grabe's third shuttle flight, but it is the first flight for Pilot Stephen Oswald. William Readdy, the flight engineer, will take over the piloting duties when the commander and pilot are sleeping.

READY FOR ANYTHING

Although they hoped they would never have to use it, the crew completed a lot of training in emergency procedures in case something should go wrong during the launch of this mission. Among other things, they practiced getting in and out of the orbiter while wearing their 41-kg (90-lb.) launch/entry suits, dropping into a water tank and climbing into a life raft.

WHAT KEEPS THE SHUTTLE FROM FALLING BACK TO EARTH?

When the shuttle is circling the Earth, it is described as being "on orbit." While it is on orbit, *Discovery* circles our planet again and again for days, traveling huge distances but using very little fuel. Have you ever wondered how exactly this is possible?

The shuttle doesn't fire its engines or use fuel to fly the way a plane does. Instead, it uses the incredible power generated at launch by its engines and the solid rocket boosters to break out of Earth's atmosphere at an amazing speed. Once on orbit, it is that speed that allows the shuttle to "fall" around the Earth.

Here's one way of thinking of it. Say you throw a baseball with all your strength. It soars upwards in a curved path because the force of your throw is greater than the force of gravity. But soon air resistance slows the ball down enough for gravity to take over. Then the ball falls back to Earth.

But hit a ball with a bat, and that stronger force carries the ball higher and farther away from its "launch pad" in another curved path. Eventually air resistance again slows the ball and gravity pulls it down.

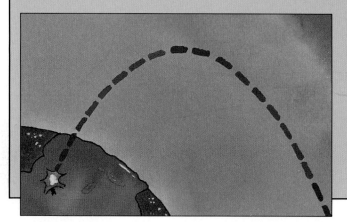

Now imagine hitting the ball so hard that it travels high enough and fast enough to break out of Earth's atmosphere. Since there is very little air resistance out there, the ball isn't slowed down and gravity has less chance to act on it. Instead of being pulled back to Earth, the ball simply keeps falling in a curved path that exactly matches the curve of our planet.

This is what is happening to the space shuttle. It is sent into the air at just the right speed — 28 000 km/h (17,500 m.p.h.). The shuttle's high speed allows it to break out of Earth's atmosphere and free-fall around the Earth in a curved path or orbit that exactly matches the planet's curve.

The shuttle's speed, 28 000 km/h (17,500 m.p.h.), is the speed that pilots call Mach 25 — 25 times the speed of sound.

Of course, little by little gravity would cause the shuttle to lose speed and fall back to Earth, not just around it. Over the course of the mission, the shuttle would fall towards Earth at a rate of about 1 km (0.5 mi.) each day.

To prevent the shuttle from this eventual falling out of orbit, the orbiter crew occasionally fire the Orbital Maneuvering System engines to correct *Discovery*'s position in space.

The shuttle would fall back even faster if it wasn't for its "attitude" or position. Once on orbit, the shuttle is turned with its tail towards Earth. In this position, the force of gravity on it is less.

As *Discovery* orbits the Earth over and over, the planet itself is rotating. With each orbit, *Discovery* passes over a slightly different area of the Earth than it did on the previous orbit. (On this orbit map, compare the orbit marked 2 and the shuttle's next pass marked 3.) In spite of this, some areas, such as Antarctica, will not be flown over at all.

◆ As soon as they are on orbit, the crew feel the first effects of being in microgravity. They seem to float, and so do any loose objects in the shuttle.

But if the shuttle crew are still within range of Earth's gravity, why do they seem to float? Because, like the shuttle itself, all the crew and cargo are traveling at such a great speed that gravity has little chance to pull them back towards Earth. So they, too, are free-falling around the planet.

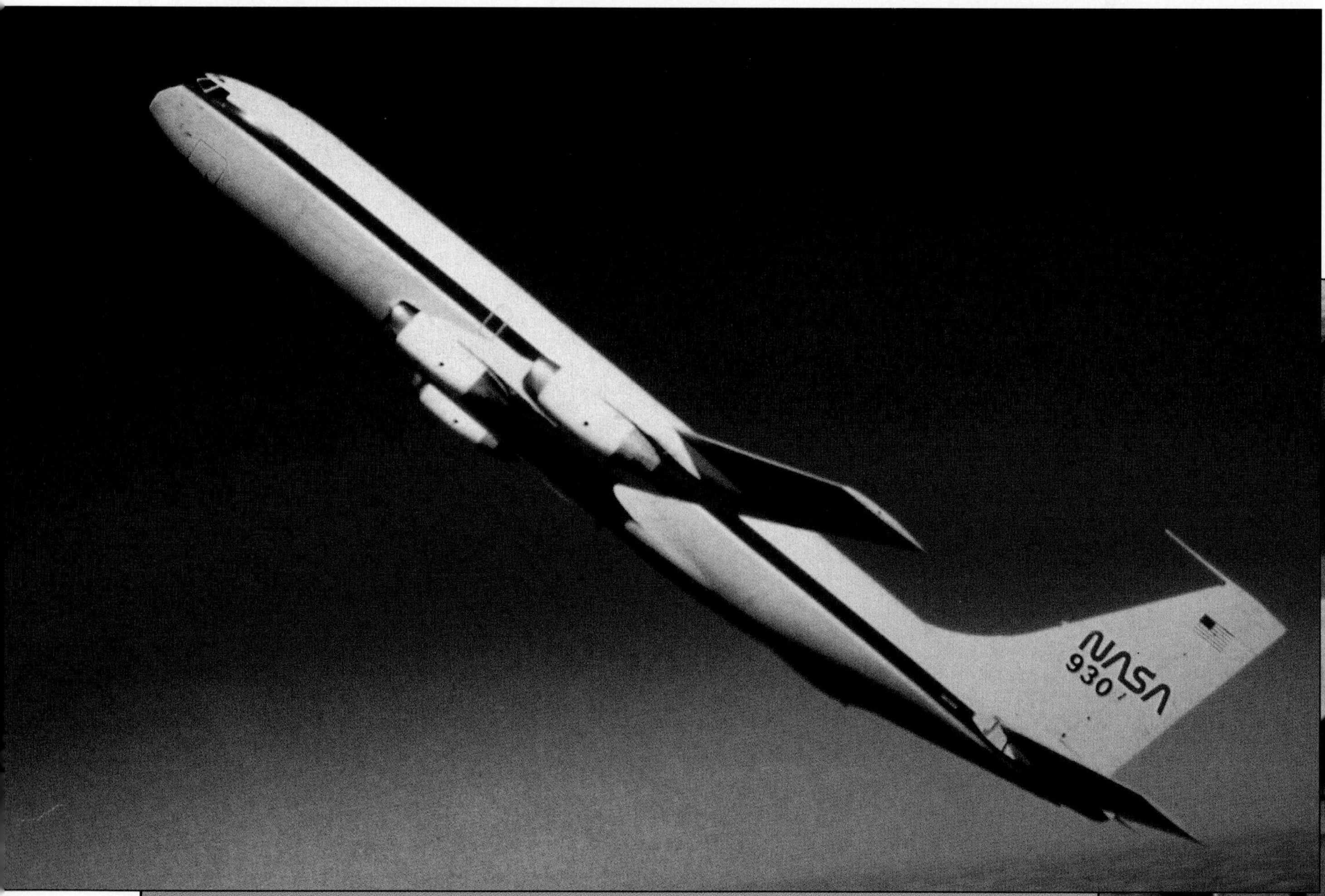

THE VOMIT COMET

Even members of the crew who haven't been in space before have experienced the feeling of weightlessness — on the KC-135 airplane. This special airplane is used to pre-test some experiments or equipment for the low gravity of shuttle flight.

As the plane climbs steeply and steadily, the acceleration increases, reaching about 2 Gs. The plane then free-falls and the passengers, like Roberta Bondar and Ken Money, shown here, feel a sense of weightlessness for 20 to 30 seconds as their seats drop out from under them.

This reduced gravity stresses many of the body's internal systems. That's why all passengers on this plane are supplied with plastic emesis bags. Because it makes its passengers sick, the KC-135 has been nicknamed "the Vomit Comet."

SHIFTING FLUIDS

uring these first several hours in space, the astronauts' bodies are undergoing a big change. On Earth, gravity pulls blood and bodily fluids down into the veins of your legs. The natural muscular tension in the legs helps out your heart in pumping the blood back up to your upper body.

In the shuttle, there is very little gravity to pull down blood and bodily fluids, but scientists think that the natural tension in the astronauts' legs continues to pump blood up to their upper bodies anyway. As a result, an astronaut's upper body gets more fluid than it needs.

Within the first six to ten hours of the flight, the astronauts' faces become puffed up by the extra fluid. Any facial wrinkles disappear. Their waistlines shrink by 2 to 5 cm (1 to 2 in.). Their shoes feel so loose, they have to tighten their laces! Eventually, much of the excess fluid is removed through the kidneys, cutting down on the total blood and fluid volume.

◆ Because of the reduced gravity, some of the crew members feel queasy. All they can do is stick a few emesis or vomit bags in their pockets and try to get their work done.

◆ During free-fall, or reduced gravity, the astronauts' arms float in front of them unless they make a conscious effort to hold them down. Later, when they leave their chairs and begin to float freely about, all their joints, such as their hips, knees, arms and elbows, will rest in a bent position. This relaxed state is called the "body-neutral" position.

◆ How fast is the shuttle travelling around the Earth? Over 8 km (5 mi.) a second! Ninety minutes after entering orbit, Discovery has already completed one circle around the Earth. The crew have seen one sunset and one sunrise in this first hour and a half — and there are lots more to come. Discovery will orbit the Earth about 16 times a day, seeing the Earth both in daylight and in darkness. At this rate they cross North America in about 10 minutes.

OUT OF THIS WORLD

◆ Once on orbit, the crew put away the temporary seats. Now they can get into some comfortable clothes and stow their launch/entry suits, but even that isn't simple on board the shuttle. It takes a long time to pack and unpack in the microgravity of the shuttle. Clothing seems to have a life of its own, floating around inside the shuttle just like the crew. Even when the astronauts use foot restraints to help them, they still can't seem to exert enough force to pack things tightly. And on this first day, it seems that every time they open a locker, clothes float free. It's a constant roundup.

◆ After putting away their suits, the astronauts get to work. With only about one week on orbit, every moment counts.

The first day's activities include activating many of the shuttle's systems: power, air pressurization, lights, communications and the bathroom.

SPACE WEAR

Space clothes have to be made a little differently from those we wear on Earth. Even the pockets have to be changed. On orbit, articles would float easily out of ordinary pockets. In the astronauts' clothes, pockets must have a seal of some kind, such as a flap with Velcro™, or elastic straps inside to hold articles in place.

When the astronauts get out of their launch/entry suits and into their clothes, they find that those clothes don't hang quite the same way they did on Earth. They float. Necklaces and shirts do not fall straight or remain close to the body. But one good thing about clothes in microgravity is that the astronauts can get both legs into their pants at the same time!

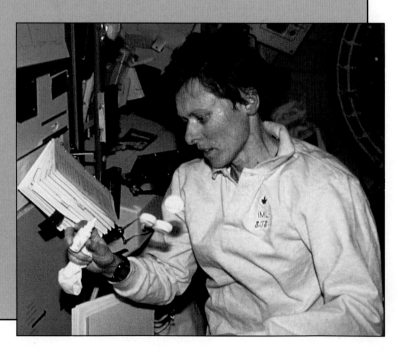

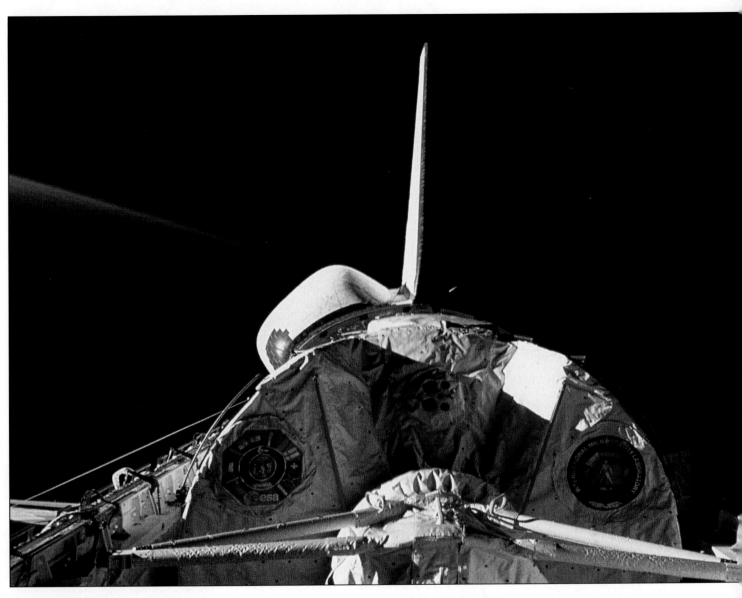

◆ About two hours after launch, Mission Specialist Norm Thagard opens the Payload Bay doors. This helps to release the heat that has built up inside the Payload Bay from the firing of the solid rocket boosters and main engines during the launch.

With the Payload Bay doors open, Spacelab is exposed to the intense heat of the sun. Beyond *Discovery*'s tail, against the dark background of space, a layer of the Earth's atmosphere gleams in the sun's light.

◆ The Payload Bay doors stay open during the whole mission to help regulate the temperature inside the orbiter. When the open Payload Bay doors face into the sunlight, the temperature outside Spacelab can be 150°C (300°F). This can cause heat to build up in the laboratory. As well, some Spacelab experiments generate heat that raises the temperature even higher. When the inside temperature gets too high, the shuttle can be rolled so its open Payload Bay doors face away from the hot sun and into dark, cold space. The outside temperature when facing in that direction might be only -100°C (-150°F). The colder outside temperature allows the shuttle to get rid of its heat, and the inside temperature drops. When it gets too cold, the orbiter rolls back the other way.

◆ With the housekeeping done, it's time to set Spacelab into action. Pilot Steve Oswald prepares to film Payload Specialist Roberta Bondar as she and Mission Specialist Norm Thagard activate the laboratory.

On the ground, this IMAX® camera weighs about 36 kg (80 lb.). In the reduced gravity of space, Steve Oswald can lift it with one hand. The series of white foot restraints on the floor help the astronauts stay in one place when they need to.

GET AWAY SPECIALS

Some experiments are not in Spacelab itself. Because these experiments don't require any attention from the Payload Specialists on board, they are located in special canisters called Get Away Special canisters behind Spacelab in the Payload Bay. Among many others, there is an experiment that will study the effects of microgravity and the sun's increased radiation on a variety of objects, including a computer floppy disk, and a special binocular telescope that will make ultraviolet observations of deep space.

◆ To enter Spacelab, the crew members "float" through the long tunnel that leads from the mid-deck of the shuttle to the rear of the payload bay. For the crew, one of the fun things about this flight is floating to work through the tunnel and coming up into a bright, humming laboratory.

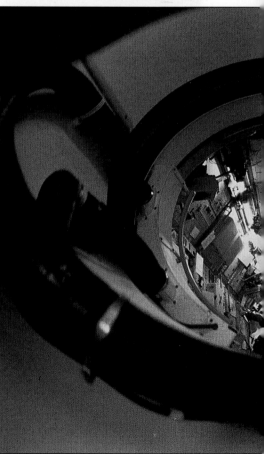

This tunnel leads from the mid-deck to Spacelab. With the Payload Bay doors open, the curved walls of the tunnel and its outer blanket are the only things separating astronauts inside from outer space.

GOLD-MEDAL SCIENCE

Many shuttles have circled or orbited the Earth. But each time a shuttle goes up on a mission, it takes many people years to prepare and costs millions of dollars. And each flight can only handle so many experiments.

The space agencies putting together the first International Microgravity Laboratory asked scientists for proposals of what should be studied in this space laboratory. They also wanted to know why the scientists thought these things should be studied, and how.

Every agency received hundreds of ideas.

Each idea was reviewed by NASA and other scientists. The reviewers wanted to choose experiments that would advance knowledge and be of value to life on Earth. To send in a proposal for such a mission is to enter the "Science Olympics." To have your experiment picked among all others to go up into space is a great achievement. It's like winning a gold medal for your event.

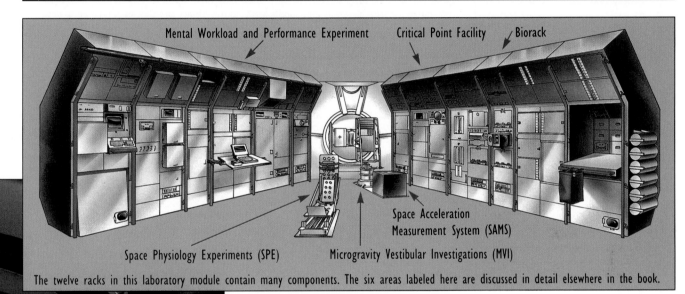

Mental Workload and Performance Experiment   Critical Point Facility   Biorack

Space Physiology Experiments (SPE)   Microgravity Vestibular Investigations (MVI)

Space Acceleration Measurement System (SAMS)

The twelve racks in this laboratory module contain many components. The six areas labeled here are discussed in detail elsewhere in the book.

In order to conduct the many experiments planned for this one mission, Spacelab's limited room is packed with banks of sophisticated, specially designed equipment running from floor to ceiling.

◆ Once Spacelab has been opened and the equipment activated, it's time to check in with the payload crew on the ground. When the experiments are under way, the ground crew will give the astronauts any advice and extra information that they can. The first conversation takes place between Payload Crew Interface Coordinator Julie Sanchez and *Discovery* Mission Specialist Norm Thagard.
Sanchez: "Spacelab, Huntsville air-to-ground. How do you read?"
Thagard: "Well, it's truly outstanding — loud and clear. How do you read?"
Sanchez: "Read you loud and clear, Norm."

GETTING TO WORK

◆ The astronauts' first full day in space begins. The two Payload and two Mission Specialists spend most of their working time in Spacelab today — and every day of the mission. They are the people in charge of all the gold-medal science experiments in space.

◆ The actual size of each astronaut's heart has changed. Because there is less gravity, blood returns from the lower body to the heart more easily than it does on Earth, flooding the upper body with more blood than is needed. As a result, the body adapts by getting rid of excess fluid through the kidneys, and the total blood volume drops. Since there is less blood to be pumped, the heart muscle itself shrinks. How much the heart shrinks varies from person to person. By this point in the mission, the astronauts' hearts are already smaller overall than they were on Earth (see diagram below).

◆ As their bodies continue to adapt to reduced gravity, the crew members feel more comfortable and work more efficiently. Concentration is important. Every minute, there are significant things to remember and do.

For example, the crew must handle potentially hazardous chemicals and hypodermic needles. They must use different kinds of cameras and videotape recorders to carefully record much of the scientific data. They must relay long, detailed mathematical readings to the ground crews. Because space inside the lab is so limited, critical pieces of equipment, such as the microscope, must be assembled each time they are used and then taken apart. Lights must be set up for photographs; seeds must be planted; loose, floating cables must be restrained; experimental containers must be moved from one compartment to another.

PRACTICE MAKES PERFECT

Over the past three years, many different science teams have been preparing experiments for the *Discovery* mission and perfecting the equipment needed to fly them into space. The Payload and Mission Specialists visited laboratories around the world, learning about each and every experiment. As the launch date drew nearer, the head of each science team came to the Marshall Space Flight Center to review, update and time parts of the experiments with the *Discovery* crew.

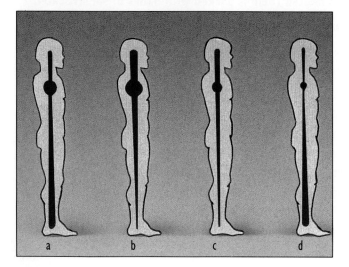

a   b   c   d

The first figure (a) shows the distribution of blood in a human body on Earth. In microgravity, more blood in the upper body causes the heart to enlarge at first (b). Then the blood volume decreases, and the heart shrinks (c). Back on Earth (d), the blood volume hasn't yet had time to increase to its normal level. The heart shrinks again and little blood gets to the upper body and brain.

TEAMMATES ON THE GROUND

Ken Money and Roger Crouch went through three years of training with Roberta Bondar and Ulf Merbold. After the first year of training, scientists Money and Crouch were chosen to be the ground-based Alternate Payload Specialists and Bondar and Merbold were chosen to be the on-board Prime Payload Specialists.

Alternate Payload Specialist Roger Crouch

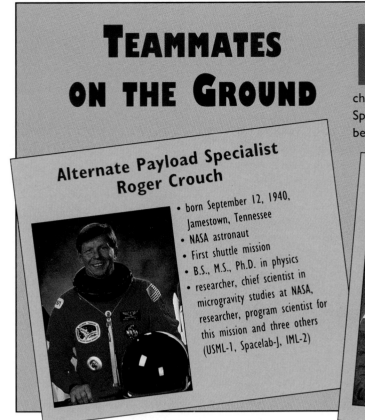

- born September 12, 1940, Jamestown, Tennessee
- NASA astronaut
- First shuttle mission
- B.S., M.S., Ph.D. in physics
- researcher, chief scientist in microgravity studies at NASA, researcher, program scientist for this mission and three others (USML-1, Spacelab-J, IML-2)

Alternate Payload Specialist Kenneth Money

- born January 4, 1935, Toronto, Ontario
- Canadian Space Agency astronaut
- First shuttle mission
- B.A. in physiology and biochemistry, M.A., Ph.D. in physiology
- pilot, former Olympic high-jumper, senior scientist at the Canadian Defence and Civil Institute of Environmental Medicine, researcher, co-investigator on inner ear experiments

Roberta Bondar and Norm Thagard peer at Earth. From these flight deck windows many useful pictures of the planet can be taken.

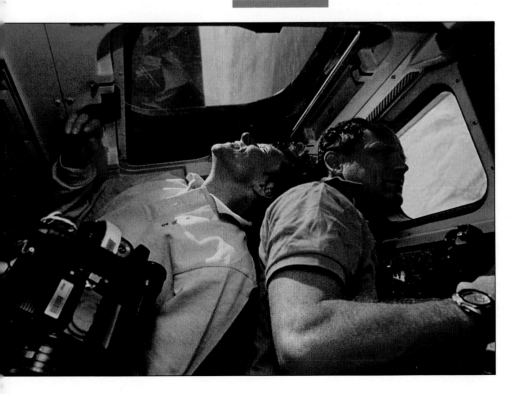

◆ The astronauts rely on a lot of help from their co-workers on Earth, especially the Alternate Payload Specialists or APSs. From the ground, the APSs (Ken Money and Roger Crouch) monitor the Prime Payload Specialists (Roberta Bondar and Ulf Merbold) minute by minute as they carry out each step of each experiment. Ken and Roger can give Ulf and Roberta immediate assistance if a piece of Spacelab equipment fails or an experiment isn't working. They contact the right scientist for instructions or brainstorm with the shuttle crew to help find a solution to the problem. And they also remind Roberta and Ulf when they should stop for lunch!

◆ You have to stand back pretty far to get a tall tree in a photo. Now imagine trying to take photographs of landforms such as a mountain range or an entire country!

That's one of the things the orbiter crew are trained to do — and today they begin to put their expertise to work. From 296 km (184 mi.) above the surface, they observe the Earth and take photographs of it with many different cameras, including IMAX. The photographs provide valuable scientific information about our planet. They help scientists on Earth calculate how well crops will grow, and they improve weather forecasting. They also enable experts to minimize soil erosion and to manage forests.

As *Discovery* orbits the planet, parts of the world are in the summer season and other parts are in the winter season. The snow and ice of winter photographs sharply reveal any large geological shapes like these volcanoes in Russia.

From the two rear windows in the flight deck shots of Earth are taken across the shuttle. At night, only city lights and natural phenomena like lightning or the northern lights are visible.

Only from space is the total size and pattern of this hurricane visible. From photos like this one, scientists can even calculate the speed of a storm's winds.

EYE IN THE SKY

IMAX cameras have been used to record thousands of metres of film on many space shuttle missions. The orbiter crew on *Discovery* are responsible for shooting the IMAX film during IML-1. They have received special training to handle the large equipment.

Developed by Canadian Graeme Ferguson, IMAX is unlike any other camera. It uses the largest-format motion picture film in the world, so it can record with much greater detail and clarity than other films. Projected onto a screen up to eight stories high, the image seems to surround you, making you feel as though you are in the picture. Take a look at how IMAX compares with other film.

| IMAX® | Standard 70 mm motion picture film | Standard 35 mm | Standard 16 mm |

◆ There is lots to do each day on board the orbiter. That's why every activity is listed on an overall daily plan called the Payload Crew Activity Plan or PCAP, pronounced "peacap." For each activity listed on the PCAP there is also a detailed checklist to lead the astronauts through it. The PCAP guides each astronaut through every minute of every hour of every day of the mission. And when the gang on the ground want to change something, a new slice of the Payload Crew Activity Plan is beamed up to the orbiter via satellite.

The upper edge has the hours numbered and divided into five-minute intervals.

The crew members are listed on the left (divided into blue shift and red shift). From left to right, the PCAP shows the activities of each astronaut throughout this six-hour period.

The single lines and triple lines in this communication section indicate when a satellite link is possible.

The Ground Track portion shows what section of the Earth the orbiter is passing over at any given moment. Notice how the path shifts slightly with each orbit.

The lower section indicates which experiments are unattended but running automatically and also which ones are using power.

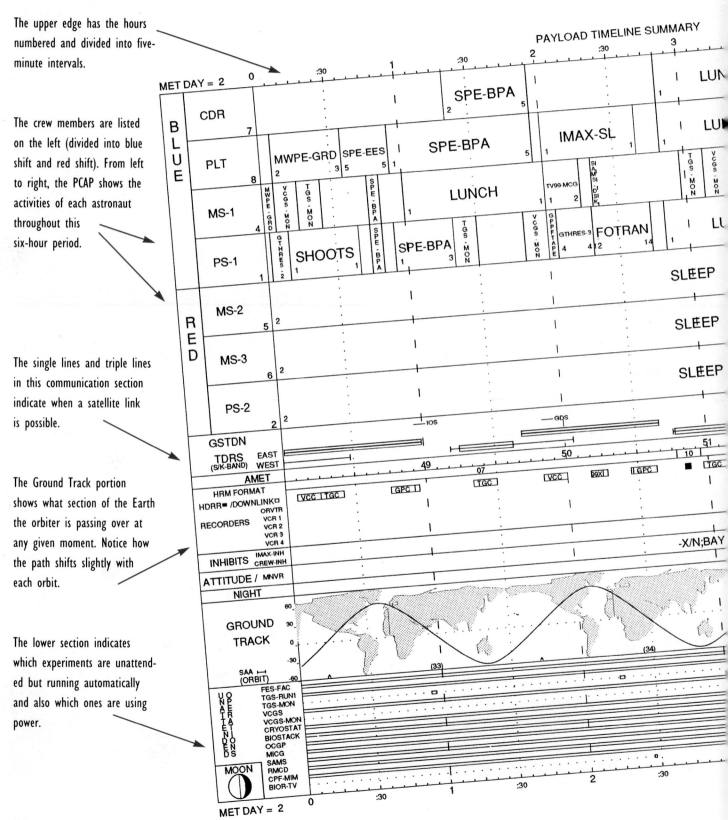

Here's Norm Thagard about to close the door to his sleeping compartment. It's right beside the washroom and galley, so to keep out the noise and light, he can use eye covers and ear plugs from his sleep kit.

CATCHING FORTY WINKS

It can be a challenge to get a good sleep on board the orbiter. Sleeping in microgravity isn't like sleeping on Earth. Air jets are necessary in each sleep compartment to blow away carbon dioxide that would otherwise accumulate around the sleeper's face. But the blowing air can actually push a sleeping astronaut around inside the compartment. To keep from being blown around too much, the astronauts try to block a few of the air jets with spare clothing. Getting into the sleep restraint or strapping on a pillow helps them avoid bumping their heads or toes. As well, the air coming in through the jets can sometimes be very chilly. Long underwear plus an extra pair of socks add some warmth.

If a crew member can't get to sleep, there is a reading light in each compartment — and the astronauts can dig into their personal lockers for the portable tape player they've packed for the trip and enjoy some music.

◆ There is no real night or day on the orbiter. Each time the shuttle circles the Earth, the crew see 45 minutes of light and 45 minutes of darkness. But the astronauts are used to night and day on Earth, so their schedules are planned with a night shift (red shift) and a day shift (blue shift), and the astronauts take turns sleeping according to their schedules. It's a good thing, too, since there aren't enough sleep compartments for all seven crew members. Instead they share the four available facilities.

SPACE AGE MUSIC

Compact discs may seem more advanced than cassette tapes to us, but they often disappoint astronauts. In many CD players, a disc must drop into place before the laser beam inside it can read the stored information and play the music. In microgravity, the disc just floats around in the compartment, preventing the laser from doing its job.

CLOSE QUARTERS

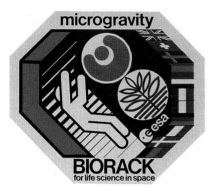

microgravity

BIORACK
for life science in space

◆ It is the second day on the orbiter, and by now, the astronauts have learned that, compared with the mid-deck and flight deck, Spacelab is a very noisy place when its big pieces of equipment are turned on.

◆ There's only so much room in Spacelab for the experiments. Take a look at the diagram of Biorack (opposite page), a biology lab that's the size of a small broom closet! Could you guess that it holds hundreds of biological specimens, such as frog eggs, fruit flies, lentil roots, slime molds, spores, stick insects, bacteria, human cells, mouse cells, nematode worms, yeast and plants? As well, it contains a freezer and cooler unit, radiation monitors, two incubators and tools. The crew carry out experiments on the specimens to help discover the effects of microgravity on other life forms.

Roberta Bondar works with plant materials inside the Biorack glovebox. As she works, her headset brings any messages or suggestions from scientists on the ground who are following her progress.

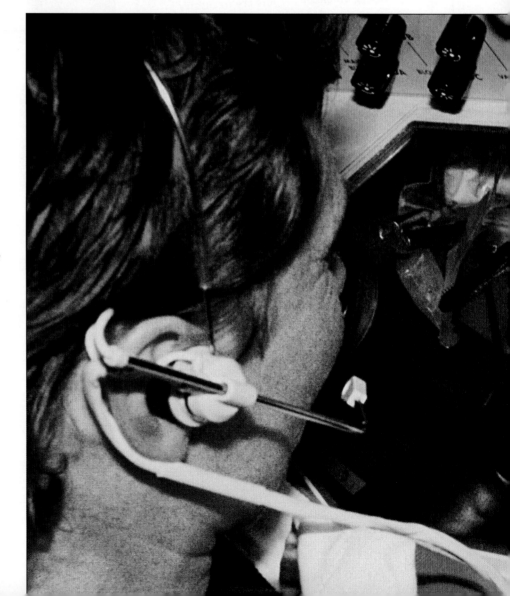

◆ Biorack also holds a glovebox. Long rubber gloves can be fitted into the holes of the glovebox to perform experiments inside it. The box keeps the experiment materials from floating too far and prevents liquids from escaping and contaminating the rest of Spacelab. A microscope can be attached to the glovebox in order to observe organisms more closely.

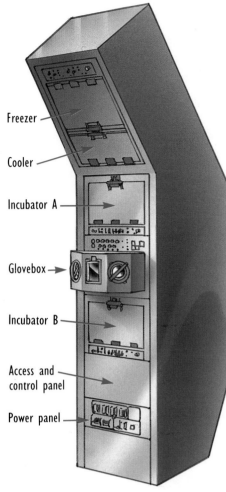

Freezer
Cooler
Incubator A
Glovebox
Incubator B
Access and control panel
Power panel

LEARNING FROM PLANTS

Plants may grow differently when they are released from Earth's gravity. In fact, scientists have reason to believe that plants may grow twice as fast and twice as large when they are grown in reduced gravity.

Why is knowing how plants behave in microgravity so important? The more we know about plants, the better we can grow our crops here on Earth. Also, when we begin to work and live in space, we will need to grow our food. We'll want to know as much as we can about how plants behave in space.

◆ On Earth, plants' roots grow down. We think this is because of gravity. Also, many plants turn to follow the light. But how do plants behave when gravity is changed? How does a plant find "down"? Can it find light without gravity? What is the smallest amount of gravity it will respond to?

To answer such questions, experiments are conducted in another lab-in-a-locker that contains centrifuges, lights, videotape recorders and plant-holding compartments. The experiments will show scientists how plants behave when they are exposed to differing amounts of light. As well, scientists will see how plants respond when placed in centrifuges that can expose the samples to differing amounts of gravity.

◆ Roberta Bondar notices that her eyesight has improved since going on orbit. No one really knows why this "space sight" occurs, but the change is so dramatic she doesn't need her glasses! Other astronauts have also noticed vision changes like this.

◆ When space is limited, it's important to be organized. To help the crew keep track of their equipment, each crew member is assigned a color that marks everything from the astronaut's drinking straw to his or her helmet.

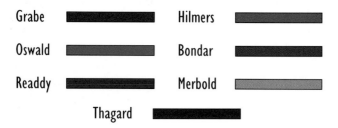

Grabe	▬▬▬▬	Hilmers	▬▬▬▬
Oswald	▬▬▬▬	Bondar	▬▬▬▬
Readdy	▬▬▬▬	Merbold	▬▬▬▬
	Thagard	▬▬▬▬	

◆ Look closely at the photos taken inside the orbiter and you'll probably notice pieces of Velcro stuck here and there. In microgravity, astronauts can't be sure that when they put an object someplace it will be there when they come back! But add Velcro, and things start to stick around. For example, a piece of Velcro attached to a pant leg is a great place to affix a food tray while an astronaut eats. The blue Velcro was put in place before launch by the

CALLING LONG-DISTANCE

"Come in, Discovery." How can such a long-distance conversation take place? Two satellites, called Tracking and Data Relay Satellites (TDRS — pronounced "teedris"), are in orbit at 35 900 km (22,300 mi.) above Earth. The satellites are positioned on different sides of Earth. Depending on the location of the shuttle, one or the other satellite is part of a space relay that links the orbiter to mission controllers on the ground. This satellite connection also allows the astronauts to relay video images electronically or "downlink" them to the people on the ground.

ground crew in places where the astronauts and engineers thought it might be useful; the yellow Velcro has been added by the IML-1 crew as they need it.

Of course, everything has its problems — even Velcro. If you accidentally backed into Velcro on a shuttle wall, you might have trouble getting free. You would have no weight to help you pry yourself loose!

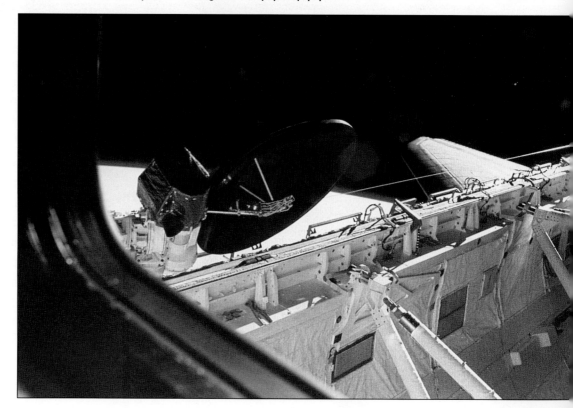

This "dish" antenna outside the Payload Bay is the orbiter's link to TDRS.

SPACE TALK

To be sure they understand one another, scientists, ground crews and orbiter crews use special expressions. You may already know some of them:

"We have lift-off" — The vehicle has lifted off the launch pad.

"Copy that"; "I copy" — I understand.

"Will do"; "Roger that"; "Affirmative" — Yes.

"That's a negative" — No.

"All systems are go" — Everything is working well.

◆ On this space shuttle flight, many press conferences are held to allow the crew to talk with important people on Earth. Today the crew receive phone calls from the President of the United States, from former astronauts and from public school students across the United States of America.

Two TDRS satellites are in orbit around Earth. A third must be put in place before continuous communication between the shuttle and the ground crew is possible. For now, the astronauts and NASA must work around the period of time in each day when neither TDRS satellite is within range for transmission.

FOOD FOR THOUGHT

This photograph and others, too, show how trash, such as the uneaten sandwiches, is disposed of in plastic bags that are stored out of the way with gray duct tape.

◆ Today Commander Ron Grabe is surprised to discover a free-floating plastic bag puffed up like a beach ball with sandwiches floating in the middle. Suddenly the crew remember that, in the excitement of the launch, they forgot to eat the sandwiches that had been packed for them.

The sandwiches look fine, but the astronauts conclude there are bacteria inside the bag. Since bacteria grow bigger and faster in space, they have produced enough gas already to make the bag puff up. The crew decide to throw away the bag and its contents: none of them wants to get food poisoning.

◆ Whenever they can, the orbiter crew roll the shuttle to keep the inside temperature comfortable. But many of the experiments on board are extremely sensitive to movement and might be affected by the shift. So often the crew must wait until they have the "all clear" to roll. As a result, the temperature inside Spacelab changes frequently. Sometimes the astronauts find it's a little too warm. Sometimes it's a little too cool. So the crew have learned to adapt, wearing only T-shirts and shorts when it's warm, at other times adding long underwear, long sleeves, pants and socks.

◆ Today, as part of the Critical Point Facility experiment, various liquids were heated. The ground-based scientists predicted that the gas that was formed would push all the remaining liquid to the outside of the test cell. But they were in for a surprise! The gas expanded in little pockets throughout the liquid.

COMING TO A BOIL

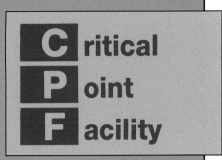

Two simple interconnected drawers are part of an orbiter experiment called the Critical Point Facility. One drawer contains a power supply and electronics. The test cells of fluid for the experiment are set up in the other drawer.

What is this experiment all about? It has to do with the critical point of fluids. The critical point is the point at which a heated fluid begins to turn to gas, as when water boils and turns into steam.

Scientists believe that all fluids act in the same way at their critical point. But they only know what happens to fluids on Earth, and on Earth, gravity "contaminates" the scientific observation of the critical point. It is gravity that causes the gas to separate from the fluid and rise. The Critical Point Facility is aboard the orbiter so that scientists can find out more about the critical point in microgravity when only temperature, not gravity, acts on the fluid.

Like much of the compact hardware scientists have developed for experiments on Spacelab, the Critical Point Facility electronics drawer is impressive. It controls the temperature of the test cells in the other drawer and can increase or decrease that temperature by the tiniest fraction of a degree — 1/1000th of a degree Celsius, to be exact.

On Earth, bubbles like these would rise to the surface of a liquid and burst. In microgravity, bubbles simply formed throughout this liquid and remained there.

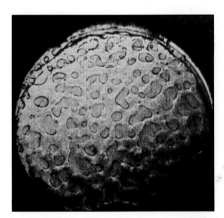

◆ When the photos were relayed electronically to the scientists who had designed the Critical Point Facility experiment, they were so excited and amazed by this new discovery, they burst into applause.

Doctors (from left) Daniel Beysens, Allen Wilkinson and Antonius Michels, Principal Investigators for the Critical Point Facility experiment, and other colleagues, respond enthusiastically to the results.

The NASA Diner

When scientists began to plan the first space flight that would carry a human being, they weren't sure if a human could even swallow food in space. No one had any experience in making food for space travel — let alone making space food taste good. So it's no wonder that the food on the first flights wasn't very appetizing.

In 1962, John Glenn carried the first NASA food for his five-hour flight around the Earth in a Mercury capsule. At the time, only a few types of food could be freeze-dried to prevent them from going bad. All his freeze-dried food was prepared in bite-sized cubes and eaten cold. In addition to the freeze-dried foods, he had other items to eat that did not have to be specially treated to keep them fresh.

The crews on the Gemini flights that began in 1965 had a greater selection of food, and light-weight plastic containers were available. Much of the food was coated in gelatin to limit crumbling and all the meals were cold, but, even so, the food tasted better than before. Now the crew could inject water into the container that contained the freeze-dried food, knead up the meal and eat it, much as they do today.

The astronauts on the three-person Apollo missions that began in 1969 had an even greater selection of food, and because hot water was now available on orbit, the crew could enjoy hot food and drinks.

When orbiter flights began in 1981, an even larger variety of foods could be rehydrated, and with the addition of heating units, the heated food was much tastier.

Lunchtime! Norm Thagard digs into a food tray to find what he wants to eat. For a hot meal, he can heat his food in the open oven up on his right.

On the walls of
the galley, silver packets of
drinking water and handy snacks
of pudding, yogurt and applesauce
are stuck to the wall
with Velcro.

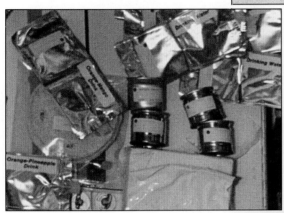

Roberta Bondar rounds up the necessary ingredients for a tortilla snack.

◆ The mid-deck of *Discovery* is about 4 m (13 ft.) by 4.5 m (15 ft.). Within this small area are the sleeping cabinets and washroom — and the crew's galley. The galley is where all the food is stored and heated. Five to eight months before the launch of IML-1, food scientists arranged food-tasting sessions. Each member of the seven-member crew chose every item for every one of their meals. The scientists evaluated the food to be sure the astronauts would be getting the proper caloric intake on the mission.

The mid-deck doesn't look much like a kitchen. Although room can be made available for a freezer or oven for experiments on the orbiter, there is no freezer or cooking oven for the crew's food. It would take up too much of the crew's living space. There is a small heating unit for warming food, though, and the galley dispenses hot or cold water.

◆ The crew won't be chowing down on any baked potatoes or steaks in the orbiter's galley. Although pieces of potato and beef can be freeze-dried and included in several of the crew's dishes, scientists haven't yet figured out how to freeze-dry large food items.

How do astronauts make a freeze-dried meal edible? First they stick a needle into a freeze-dried food pack and inject a pre-selected amount of hot or cold water. Then they knead or shake the food until it is thoroughly moistened. Next the astronauts snip around the plastic with surgical scissors to make an opening big enough for a spoon — and then it's time to dig in.

◆ "The sauce is loose!" The alert comes from Roberta Bondar, who has let the shrimp cocktail sauce lose contact with her spoon.

Food particles of any kind can be a problem in microgravity. They don't drop to the ground. Until they are recaptured, they hang in the air and could be dangerous if they find their way into someone's eye, nose or ear. They can also infect and ruin experiments and interrupt electrical circuits. To be safe, most of the solid food sent into space is naturally moist. The moister the food, the fewer the crumbs. Luckily, food escapes didn't happen very often on this flight.

◆ There are no baked beans or large amounts of broccoli or mushrooms on the crew's menu. Why not? They might cause the crew to experience gas pains. Gas pains are more painful in space and could be potentially dangerous as scientists still aren't sure how gases behave in microgravity.

◆ What are the crew's favorite meals? Shrimp cocktail with sauce, tortillas with peanut butter or cheese spreads, and chicken dishes. Items from the fresh food locker are pretty popular, too. The day before lift-off, it's packed with candies, sweets and snacks, relish, cookies, chewing gum and apples.

SPACE SPOONS

Because most foods contain water, and in microgravity water tends to stick like jelly to most surfaces, it's easy to load food on spoons in space. In fact, that explains why the spoons on the orbiter don't have to be as big as Earth spoons — in microgravity, the food sticks to both sides!

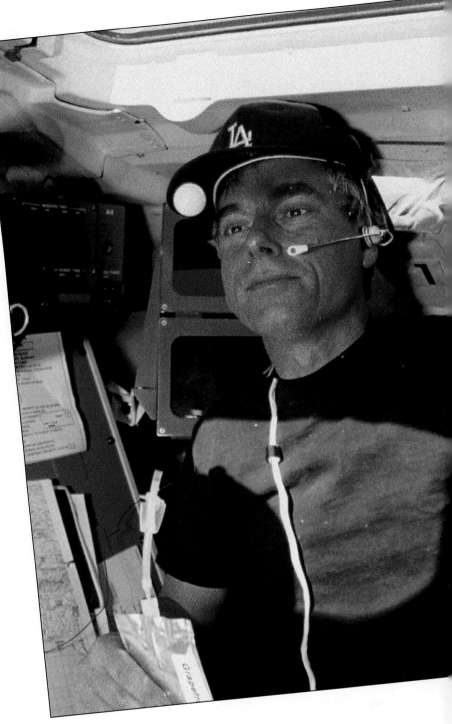

Ulf Merbold examines a perfect sphere of floating grapefruit juice he has squeezed from his juice bag. On Earth, when juice is spilled, the drops aren't spherical. They're teardrop-shaped.

On a previous mission,
astronaut Joe Allen demonstrated
the space-age way to drink orange juice.
He squeezes a small amount of juice from the
juice package (top). Because of the lack of gravity, it
simply floats as a sphere. Once he manages to insert
his drinking straw, he just sucks it up. The
sphere gets smaller until it's all gone.

◆ Space is a great place to play with your food. In microgravity, the astronauts can twirl carrot sticks, swallow a floating sphere of sauce and send a half-peeled banana spinning across the mid-deck with its peel sticking out like propeller blades.

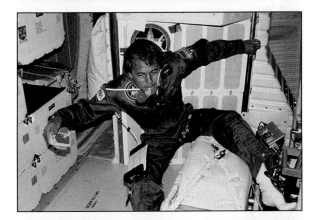

WHAT GIVES A TEARDROP ITS SHAPE?

Why are drops of juice on Earth teardrop-shaped and drops on the orbiter sphere-shaped? First of all, small amounts of fluid form drops because of surface tension. The molecules under the surface of a fluid pull on the molecules near the surface of the water. It is as if the surface of the fluid forms a "skin" that prevents molecules from escaping from the liquid. The fluid forms a drop or bubble.

If we could look closely at juice falling from a cup on Earth in slow motion, we would see that the drop begins as a sphere, perfectly round. Then gravity pulls on the juice, giving it weight. The weight of the juice lengthens the sphere and it becomes teardrop-shaped.

And in the microgravity of the orbiter? When juice escapes from a container, it forms a sphere — and remains a sphere.

When Up Isn't Up

◆ The crew is full of excitement today. They have just learned that the mission is going to be extended by a day.

The decision was based on many factors. The use of power on IML-1 has been kept to a minimum, so there is still some left. All the orbiter facilities and computer systems are running beautifully. The superb efforts and round-the-clock productivity of the orbiter crew have produced great amounts of reliable data, much more than expected, and the teamwork of the on-orbit and ground-based crews is running smoothly. Everyone begins planning for an extra day's activities, making lists of experiments that could be lengthened or repeated to gain extra data.

◆ On the orbiter is an area called the Mental Workload and Performance Experiment station. A rack at this station holds a computer workstation with an adjustable tabletop, joystick and trackball. Scientists hope experiments with the station will help them to design workstations that are more functional, more comfortable and better suited to working in space.

Six of the seven IML-1 crew members cram into Spacelab as they try to get their work done.

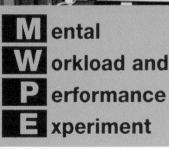

Mental
Workload and
Performance
Experiment

◆ All the crew members are tested at the MWPE station in Earth's gravity before the shuttle flight and in microgravity during the flight. Today the computer is measuring Commander Ron Grabe's speed and responses as he performs various tasks on the computer. The foot restraints keep him from floating away.

More tests will be done when the flight is finished. The computer will compare the in-flight results to the crew members' other scores.

Ron Grabe works at the Mental Workload and Performance Experiment station. His left arm, not in use, hangs in the body-neutral position that is typical in microgravity.

FIT AS A FIDDLE

Daily exercise is important aboard the orbiter. When gravity is reduced, there is no force against which the astronauts can exert their muscles. This means they don't need to use their muscles very much. But muscles and bones that aren't used can deteriorate quickly. Daily exercise helps the astronauts maintain some tone in their muscles, bones and cardiovascular system, which will also help them readjust more quickly when they return to Earth's gravity. A rowing machine, modified for use in microgravity, was taken up on this mission and used by the orbiter crew so scientists could assess its usefulness for keeping fit in space.

◆ After a long, hard day's work, the astronauts might look forward to a shower. But they won't find one on the orbiter. Without much gravity to draw the water to the floor, the water would float about the room. So how do the crew members keep clean?

Sponge baths. Or towel baths, really. Trying to use as little water as possible, they soak a towel with a water gun and use it to get wet. Then they soak another towel with soapy water from a body rinse bag to wash themselves. Except for its label, the body rinse bag looks like a regular drinking water bag with its straw and clamp — so the astronauts try not to get confused! Another wet towel rinses off the soap, and the bath is complete.

◆ To clean their hair, astronauts use a wet, rinseless shampoo. They apply the shampoo, taking care not to stir up soap bubbles, which will be difficult to get out of the air. Then they towel their hair to dry it. The astronauts have learned not to bother spending much time combing their hair. In microgravity, hair quickly floats out of place.

◆ Ever wonder how astronauts use a toilet in microgravity? The toilet on the orbiter has foot and thigh restraints and hand holds so that the astronauts can prevent themselves from floating away from the toilet while they are using it. The toilet doesn't flush. Instead, a fan creates an air current that pulls the solid waste down to a compartment where it is dried and disinfected. Liquid waste is drawn into a funnel, then run through some flexible tubing and finally pumped into the wastewater tank.

◆ Brushing your teeth on orbit is pretty much the same as on Earth, except that the astronauts must either swallow the toothpaste or spit it into a cloth.

LOOK MA, NO CAVITIES

Can you imagine having a toothache while traveling high out of reach of your dentist on Earth? So far, none of the astronauts have had any complaints. That may be because they all must have their tooth fillings checked by NASA dentists before the mission to ensure there are no air pockets under them. If there had been, the fillings would have been replaced. Why? Sudden drops in pressure that occur in space environments allow air to expand. If that air is trapped under a filling, the expanding air presses on sensitive tooth nerves, causing pain.

RUB-A-DUB-DUB

On Earth, when you wash your face, water molecules adhere, or stick, to molecules on your skin. When you shake yourself off, you break some of the adhesion, or sticking force, that is holding the water and skin molecules together. Gravity pulls to the floor any water droplets that were shaken loose. And on the shuttle?

Pilot Steve Oswald is demonstrating a microgravity eyewash. The liquid he is using to soothe his sore eyes is contained in a pair of goggles. At first the liquid sticks to Steve's eyes like jelly. When Steve shakes his head to free his eyes, the liquid separates from his eyes — but gravity doesn't pull it down and out of the way. As Steve continues shaking his head — smack! He gets a faceful of floating eyewash.

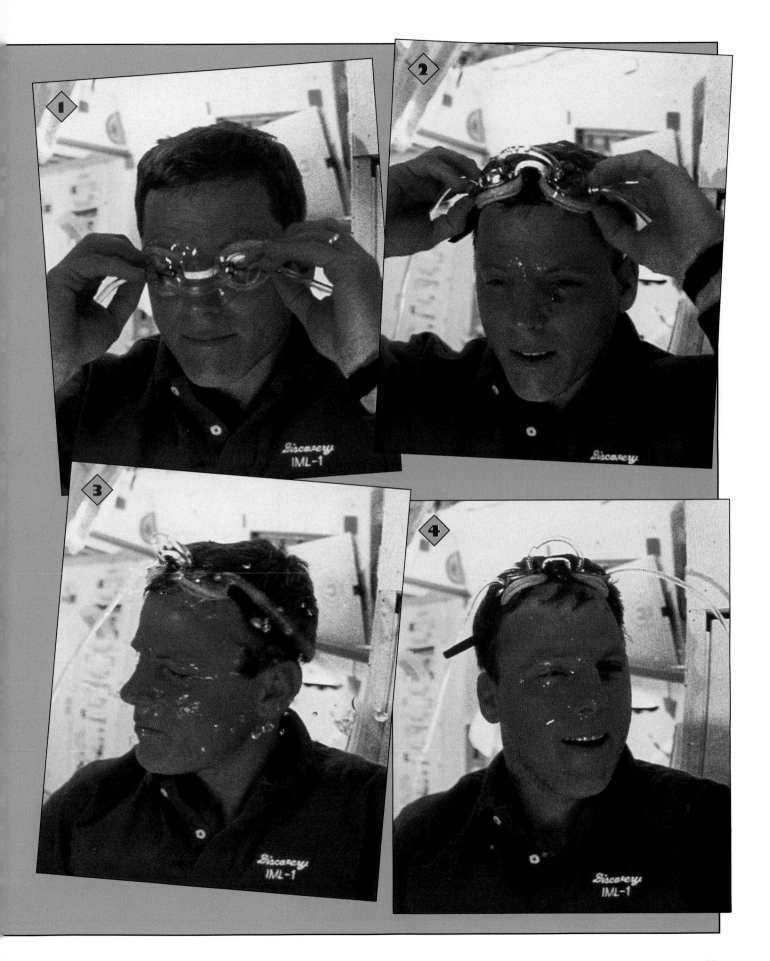

ON A ROLL

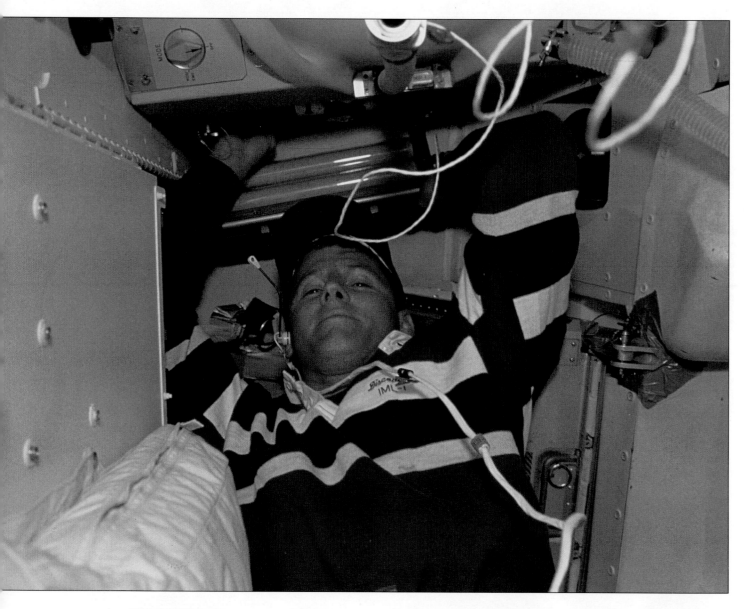

Housekeeping tasks fill any spare moments the crew members might have. Pilot Stephen Oswald avoids floating cables as he replaces some light tubes.

◆ This is the fifth day in space, and the crew members have learned that when they're not working — they're working. Often 18 hours each day. Just keeping the orbiter clean and operational is a continuous task. There are air filters to clean and change. There is food to prepare. There is trash to stow. The extra water produced by the fuel cells has to be pumped out the back of the shuttle. And of course there are always reports to send to the ground crew.

With all of the photographs scheduled to be taken throughout the mission, it's important to have the numerous cameras loaded and ready. Here Bill Readdy gets the many types of film organized in preparation for the next batch of shots.

SPACE ACCELERATION
MEASUREMENT SYSTEM

NASA
Lewis Research Center
Cleveland, Ohio

◆ Some of the experiments in Space-lab are so sensitive that they are influenced by the firings of the orbiter's engines — and even by vibrations in the orbiter from crew activity! That's why the Space Acceleration Measurement System unit is on board. About the size of a briefcase, this unit measures and records accelerations and changes in the orbiter's motions. These records will help the scientists determine if vibrations might have affected the results of some experiments.

◆ Today Payload Specialist Ulf Merbold speaks in German and English to the Director General of the European Space Agency. Commander Ron Grabe, who also speaks German, joins in the conversation. Payload Specialist Roberta Bondar chats in French and English with the Canadian Prime Minister, who offers congratulations for the great job she and the crew are doing on their mission.

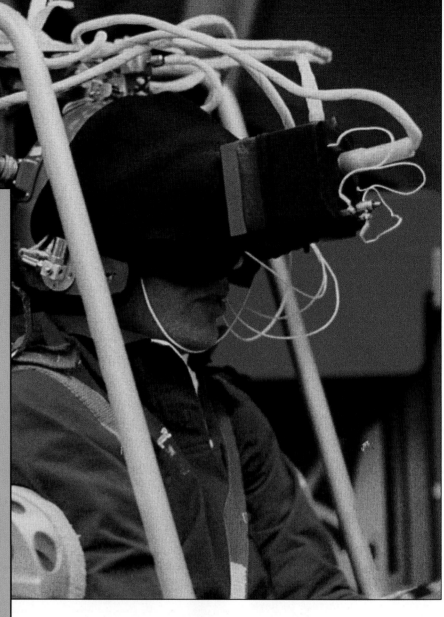

OUR AMAZING INNER EAR

The Microgravity Vestibular Investigations test an astronaut's inner ear. The inner ear is like the body's own Space Acceleration Measurement System (see page 47). It is made up of hairs, tiny bones, cartilage and liquid. The semicircular canals — the vestibular system of the inner ear — help the body sense angular acceleration (acceleration along a curved path). Your eyes contribute more information, and your brain also receives signals from other cells and body tissues.

Scientists aren't sure what part the vestibular system plays in causing motion sickness. They hope that studying the vestibular system in microgravity will help them learn what parts of the system contribute to motion sickness or other inner-ear illnesses and find ways to prevent them.

Dave Hilmers sits in the MVI chair.

His complicated headgear records the movement of his eyes

as he is spun rapidly in one of three directions.

◆ Dave Hilmers is all dressed and ready to ride on the Microgravity Vestibular Investigations chair. Rotating around as though on some wild amusement park ride can produce nausea, however.

So why do it? This experiment is an investigation of how the body adapts to weightlessness. In particular, it explores the role of the inner ear or vestibular system in detecting motion and pressure changes.

The crew take vestibular tests before the flight and during the flight. They'll take more tests after the flight, too. By comparing the results of all of these tests, investigators hope to learn more about gravity's effect on the vestibular system.

◆ Crew members are tested in one of three positions during the Microgravity Vestibular Investigations:

Rotating motion is called roll.

Up-and-down motion is called pitch.

Side-to-side motion is called yaw.

◆ Take a look at Dave Hilmers's headgear. It contains an infrared camera that records his eye movements.

What do the eyes have to do with balance? Without a healthy vestibular system, the eyes don't work properly. The vestibular system stabilizes the eyes so that images do not become blurred. Also, the brain uses information both from the eyes and from the inner ears when it is determining the body's movement and position. The brain checks information from the inner ear against information from the eyes. In situations such as microgravity, the brain may start to rely more on what the eye is seeing and less on data from the ear.

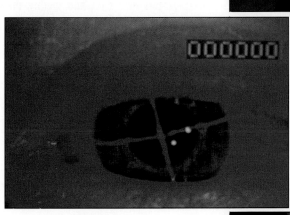

A special lens is placed on Roberta Bondar's eyeball. Its crosshair gives the camera within the MVI headgear a point of focus to track as the eye moves.

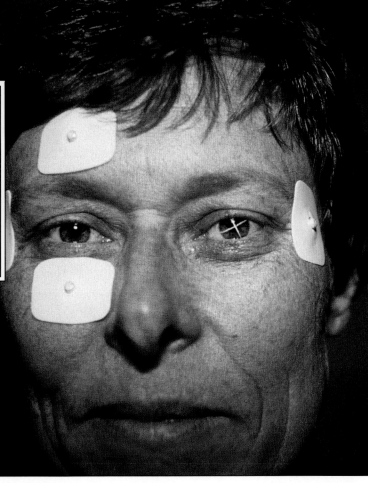

SCRAMBLED SENSES

Roberta Bondar sits with eyes closed as Norm Thagard records her responses throughout the proprioception experiment.

◆ Today is the extra day added to the mission. A new piece of Payload Crew Activity Plan is sent up to *Discovery*. The day will be spent repeating experiments like these Space Physiology Experiments to get even more data.

◆ One test examines Roberta Bondar's proprioception, or sense of body position. On Earth, the inner ear and nerve endings in our joints and muscles give us a sense of which way is up. Our eyes also help us figure it out. In space, with their eyes closed, the astronauts sometimes have a tough time figuring out things like whether their arm is above their head or below it. Scientists aren't sure why that is.

◆ In another experiment, Dave Hilmers sits in a sled chair as Ulf Merbold slides it back and forth on rails. On Earth, the inner ear provides a sense of up and down. The nervous system, including the brain, uses this information to send signals to various parts of the body, telling them how to respond based on their current position. This all takes place because gravity is acting on the inner ear.

But what happens when there is no gravity, no up or down? The organs of the inner ear send different information. The nervous system must learn to interpret this new data and modify the signals it sends out. The sled tests the body's responses to linear motion in microgravity. The test measures changes in the organs of the inner ear as the astronaut moves quickly forward, and it tries to determine how long the brain takes to respond and readapt to the situation in order to send correct messages to the body.

Dave Hilmers sits strapped into the sled chair as Ulf Merbold sends it sliding back and forth.

50

**Dave Hilmers sits before
the rotating dome of another SPE.**

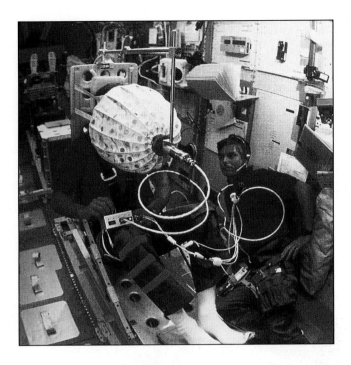

◆ During the rotating dome SPE, information from both the eye and the inner ear is received by the brain. Measuring the astronaut's response to the rotating set of dots on the dome and the reaction of his balance system will help scientists understand whether, in space, either the eye or the inner ear gives the brain more useful information.

◆ The astronauts' bodies began to adjust to microgravity within hours after going into orbit. Over the course of the mission, a series of Space Physiology Experiments are carried out to learn more about the fluid shift and other physiological changes that take place.

Today, like every day, the astronauts' calves are measured to track how blood pools in the legs during reentry from space. The study will help improve pressure suits, which are worn to decrease the amount of pooling. It will also help scientists improve other devices that help return blood to the heart and brain. These may aid pilots, divers and people with circulation problems and paralysis.

**Steve Oswald's calf is
measured to help record how fluid shifts
within astronauts' bodies when they move from
gravity to microgravity and then
back to gravity.**

◆ Today the crew has its worldwide press conference, which is downlinked to Earth. During the conference, Commander Grabe dedicates the flight to Sonny Carter. During the flight, the crew have been taking turns wearing Sonny's favorite baseball cap and remembering the Mission Specialist.

For the press conference, the entire crew gathers in Spacelab. As they cluster in the small laboratory, it's clear that in space there really is no up or down.

LIGHTS, CAMERA, ACTION!

Like all other investigation teams, the IMAX crew members work shifts around the clock to match the efforts of the shuttle crew. They are constantly watching the color monitors that show *Discovery*'s flight path and assessing which astronaut is available to shoot some film footage. They are also keeping one eye on a detailed weather report. It helps them determine the cloud cover over a section of the Earth before the orbiter passes over it. Although the locations to be filmed from the orbiter have been chosen months or even years before this flight, the speed and path of the orbiter allows only two filming opportunities for any location. If clouds cover the area for long, the opportunity is missed.

◆ Meanwhile, back on Earth, members of the IMAX crew are hard at work. In the IMAX pod at the Marshall Space Flight Center, Graeme and Phyllis Ferguson are planning some shots of Earth from the shuttle with crew trainer Jim Neihouse.

IMAX team members Graeme Ferguson (left), Phyllis Ferguson and Jim Neihouse considering the next area to be filmed.

◆ It's good teamwork that is making IML-1 a successful mission. The crews on Earth — the science crews, communications crews, flight crews, training crews and technical operations crews — are all working with the shuttle crew like finely tuned pieces in a mammoth three-dimensional moving jigsaw puzzle.

WINDING DOWN

WHAT IS A CRYSTAL?

C rystals can be made from many different types of materials. Look at table salt through a hand lens and you'll be looking at salt crystals like these. All crystals are made of atoms that are arranged in neat, regular patterns. When crystals grow, additional atoms of the same type attach themselves to form more and more neat, regular layers.

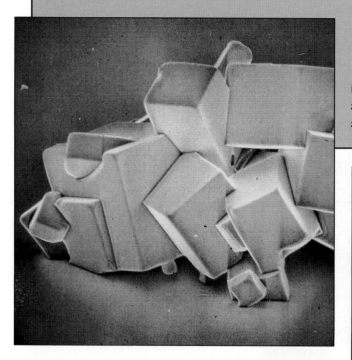

◆ The shuttle crew have been growing crystals ever since they went into orbit. When crystals are grown on Earth, their own weight often makes them develop flaws. Some crystals can't even be grown large enough for scientists to examine and understand their structure. Crystal experiments on previous shuttle flights showed that crystals grow faster, larger and with fewer defects in microgravity.

Today, the IML-1 crew downlink some "live action" video of crystal growth. The scientists on the ground are able to watch the crystal growth as it occurs in Spacelab.

In space, the reduced gravity allows crystals, like this chunk of mercury iodide, to grow faster, larger and with fewer defects. On the IML-1 mission, the largest-ever mercury iodide crystal was produced.

HELPFUL SPACE CRYSTALS

The crystals grown on the International Microgravity Laboratory will be put to good use on Earth.

❑ The mercury iodide crystals will help detect harmful gamma rays in nuclear power plants and nuclear medicine centers.

❑ Triglycine sulfate crystals will be used as infrared heat detectors in telescopes, Earth observation cameras, forest fire detectors and security systems.

❑ Some complex nickel compounds will be grown in space to be used as superconductors on Earth. Superconductors conduct electric current with great efficiency because they waste little energy. They are used in computers, communications satellites and many other electrical devices.

❑ Gamma-interferon crystals grown on this mission will be used to stimulate the human immune system to treat certain cancers.

❑ A number of other crystals grown on the shuttle may provide a better understanding of seed and plant proteins, as well as virus and enzyme structures, when scientists study them further on Earth.

Roberta Bondar examines the progress of a large mercury iodide crystal growing in a special "furnace" within Spacelab.

◆ By the end of the eight days, the astronauts' height has increased by 2 to 5 cm (1 to 2 in.) because there is no gravity pulling down on their spines.

◆ In just over a day, *Discovery* will be touching down at Edwards Air Force Base in California. The orbiter crew begin deorbit preparation. The rest of the crew begin to pack up. They must restow over 1,000 objects, such as the equipment in Spacelab and their own clothes — and it isn't easy in microgravity. Anything that is left floating around could hurt someone or interfere with controls when gravity brings it crashing down.

Commander Grabe has become handy with the camera. Here he is getting ready to take another shot from the two small windows at the rear of the flight deck.

◆ How many astronauts does it take to close a drawer? In microgravity, three. Once the many boxes of plant samples are replaced in the Biorack drawer, Roberta pushes against "the ceiling" with her arms so her feet will press the lid down. Steve and Norm fasten the clasps.

Then they deactivate the equipment, stow the specimens and instruments, and gather up the cards on which they have recorded their notes.

◆ While cleaning up, Roberta comes upon her glasses, which have floated from Spacelab through the tunnel and into the mid-deck. Because her "space sight" or improved vision lasted for the entire flight, she hasn't needed to wear them or even noticed that they were missing.

With the mission complete, the Payload Bay doors are closed to prepare for *Discovery*'s return to Earth.

◆ After checking compartment by compartment, the Mission Specialists and the Payload Specialists are responsible for closing down and deactivating Spacelab. The tunnel is then sealed off to protect the scientific samples, and the crew safely stow in the mid-deck any objects that wouldn't fit in Spacelab itself.

◆ A member of the orbiter crew closes the Payload Bay doors to cover Spacelab and the Get Away Special canisters.

COMING HOME

◆ Now it's just a matter of hours to touchdown. In preparation, the crew put the take-down seats that were stowed away after the launch back into place in the mid-deck and the flight deck.

◆ Mission Specialist David Hilmers and Payload Specialist Roberta Bondar take blood pressure readings on each other. These two crew members volunteered to undergo continuous monitoring of their blood pressure and heart rate during *Discovery*'s return to Earth. This will give scientists even more data on the human body's reactions to the change in gravity.

FALLING FROM THE SKY

Taking an orbiter out of orbit is not as easy as you'd think. In order to fall back to Earth and land in the right spot, the orbiter has to leave orbit at exactly the right time and place. Otherwise, who knows where they might end up.

The first step to leaving orbit goes off without a hitch. Pilot Oswald turns *Discovery* so its tail faces the sun and its nose points back to Earth. The Orbital Maneuvering System engines fire to slow the orbiter just enough so that gravity begins to have more of an effect on it. Gravity pulls *Discovery* out of orbit towards Earth in a gentle glide. From now until after Mach 1, the speed of sound, the orbiter is flown almost completely by the on-board computer, although the orbiter crew keep a close eye on things and make adjustments when they are called up from the ground by Mission Control.

◆ It won't be easy for the astronauts' cardiovascular systems to readapt to gravity. When they left Earth, their blood volume decreased to adapt to the microgravity of the shuttle flight — and now their blood volume needs to increase again as they deorbit.

To avoid feeling thirsty and lightheaded once back in Earth's gravity, the crew members try to help their bodies rebuild their blood volume. They drink as much liquid as they can one hour before reentry — about four to eight drink bags each. They also take salt tablets. The salt tablets help their bodies retain the fluid. More drink bags and salt tablets are prepared to have ready to drink during the trip back to Earth.

◆ Meanwhile, down on the ground, a crowd of people wait. Before dawn today, the families and friends of the crew drove in a convoy of cars through the desert to the Edwards Air Force Base. Shortly before touchdown, they will be escorted to a roof from which they can get the best view of the shuttle landing.

◆ With about an hour remaining before touchdown, the crew get into their launch/entry suits. They strap themselves into position in their assigned seats for reentry. Helmets are locked securely into place.

◆ All suited up and strapped into their seats, the crew keep eating salt tablets and drinking to get their blood volume back up to levels appropriate for Earth's gravity.

Commander Ronald Grabe and Pilot Stephen Oswald are dressed for reentry and eager to take their crew home.

◆ Soon after the orbiter begins its return to the Earth, the force of gravity inside the shuttle begins to increase. At only two-tenths of what we consider normal gravity, or Earth's gravity, the drink bags stop floating and drop towards the floor.

◆ The crew notice their bodies feeling heavy. Then they experience the full force of reentry. They had felt 3 Gs during the launch because they were lying on their backs, moving straight up out of the Earth's gravity, fighting against its force. Now, they are gliding back towards the Earth's gravitational pull and coming in at an angle, so they feel only 2 Gs of gravity. But the force of 2 Gs feels heavier than the 3 Gs at launch did. This is because the astronauts' bodies have weighed nothing for a week.

◆ The crew feel the aerodynamic changes around *Discovery*. The orbiter vibrates as the friction from Earth's atmosphere causes it to slow from orbiting speed, 25 times the speed of sound, to 2 times the speed of sound. The astronauts feel the drop in speed as a tugging at their safety harnesses. About two minutes before landing, the orbiter has dropped to a speed of 1.2 times the speed of sound and begins to break through the sound barrier. The astronauts feel as if the orbiter is going through turbulence. This is called buffeting.

◆ As the orbiter reaches Mach 1, the speed of sound, about 15 km (9.3 mi.) from the surface of the Earth, Commander Grabe and Pilot Oswald gradually take over full control from the computers and prepare to land the orbiter. They must glide to the ground in a single attempt. *Discovery* has no power of its own and can't come around again for a second try. As if that isn't tricky enough, the orbiter must land softly so that all the valuable specimens and film aren't destroyed.

◆ Just before the people on the ground see *Discovery*, they hear two loud booms. This is the nose — and then the tail — of the orbiter breaking the sound barrier as the orbiter slows down from Mach 1 to below the speed of sound.

GETTING USED TO GRAVITY

If you've ever been sick in bed for a week, you know that when you get up for the first time, your legs are wobbly, your pulse is high, and you feel unsteady. This is the way the astronauts feel after being in microgravity for over one week. In just eight days, they have become so conditioned to microgravity that their bodies will have to readjust to living in 1 G.

Readaptation to Earth is very strenuous. In the week after they return, the crew will gradually — and carefully — increase their amount of exercise until their hearts regain their pre-flight size and strength. It will probably take them up to a week before their balance and fine motor skills are back to what they were before the mission.

Scientists hope to learn more about the physical deconditioning process that takes place in space so they can figure out ways to lessen its impact.

◆ The orbiter touches down at 360 km/h (224 m.p.h.). As the first trail of dust rises from the rear wheels, the crowd cheers and screams with relief and joy.

◆ Family members are escorted to the clinic where the crew will be checked out. Family and friends, tourists and media reporters all strain for their first sight of the crew.

But the crew don't appear right away. They have a long orbiter shutdown checklist to go through when they land. The crew check for toxic gases from unused fuel for the Orbital Maneuvering System, they turn off the equipment on board — and they try to get their "Earth legs" in shape. After eight days without gravity, this isn't easy — especially while they are wearing 41-kg (90-lb.) launch/entry suits.

◆ The crew transport vehicle moves in. Just under one hour after landing, the crew leave the orbiter by the side hatch and climb aboard. The crew change out of their launch/entry suits and, for the first time in over a week, have a drink of water without using a straw. Each crew member is examined by flight surgeons on the crew transport vehicle.

◆ The transport vehicle takes the crew members to the clinic at Edwards Air Force Base. Here each astronaut finally stands on the ground once more — and receives hugs from relieved family members and friends.

This special transport van rises up to allow the astronauts easy access from the shuttle. Then it safely lowers them to ground level and speeds them towards Edwards Air Force Base.

◆ Inside the clinic, the astronauts are checked out more thoroughly by the flight surgeons and the four Specialists begin their post-flight testing. By the end of the day, the crew members are back with their families, eating dinner together and enjoying being back on the ground.

THE CONTINUING SAGA

SPACE TECHNOLOGY IN OUR LIVES

Experiments and the experience of living on space shuttle flights have resulted in many direct benefits to life on Earth. Each year NASA publishes a special book describing spin-offs from space technology so people can learn what new technology or materials are available and what products are being made from them. Here is a small part of an ever-growing list of items originally created for space use.

- rehydratable foods
- special foam for ski boots, football pads, helmets, hospital bed pads
- thermal gloves, boots and blankets
- equipment for better prediction of global weather and climate change
- smoke detectors
- microcomputers
- cushioning used in athletic shoes

- stick controls for disabled drivers
- technology to develop liquid-cooled garments for use in space outside the orbiter, also used in thermal control in cancer therapy and spinal cord injury
- cordless drills and other tools
- defogging gel for glasses
- scratch-resistant coatings for plastic lenses

- a hand-held, low-intensity X-ray imager, called a lixiscope, used for small children in emergency rooms, bedridden patients, accident victims and injured sports players

◆ The flight may be over — but the work isn't. In the weeks that follow the landing, the International Microgravity Laboratory crew go through intensive post-flight tests. The scientists are interested in discovering as much as they can about human bodies that have just spent eight days in space.

Monitoring the astronauts aboard shuttle flights and once they've returned to Earth has helped scientists learn more about things like back pain, blood flow in the brain and how the inner ear works. Some data from space is helping doctors treat children with certain bone deficiencies and may help adults to fight osteoporosis, a disease that causes bone loss.

◆ The Payload and Mission Specialists also work hard with the scientists at long debriefing sessions. They go over all their notes for each of the experiments. They discuss what went well, what didn't, and how future procedures and training could be improved.

◆ After preliminary analysis, some of the data from this *Discovery* mission will be released to fellow scientists. Information from other experiments will take years to analyze before it is released. And there are always more questions. In fact, some IML-1 scientists have already booked space in the lab of future shuttle flights to continue trying to answer their questions.

◆ When the medical testing and debriefing are completed, the orbiter crew and Mission Specialists are reassigned to future flights. The Payload Specialists prepare to continue in their country's astronaut program or pursue their own research.

◆ Astronauts, whether they are orbiter crew members, Mission Specialists or Payload Specialists, are a very special breed. Do you want to be an astronaut? Here are some words of advice from some of the *Discovery* astronauts.

Ron Grabe: "Pursue a broad range of interests until the time you have sampled enough areas to really know when you find the one that interests you most."

Norman Thagard: "You need to have goals and take risks to achieve them. Be the best you can be at whatever you choose."

Sonny Carter: "You can do or be anything you want to. Expect success, not failure."

Dave Hilmers: "Choose what you really like to do. There is lots of luck involved with being an astronaut. Entering space is not the most important part of the job."

◆ Why is what astronauts do so important? Here's what a few of the IML-1 astronauts think.

Roberta Bondar: "It's important to advance the use of space as a new environment for science, to answer questions we can't answer on Earth."

Steve Oswald: "The value of knowledge gained by the shuttle program has real application to bettering life on Earth."

Norman Thagard: "If we lose our frontiers, we lose our drive and our incentives."

INDEX